THE CLIP ART CAROUSEL
All-Purpose Art

Written & Illustrated by Beverly Armstrong

The Learning Works

Copyright © 1986
The Learning Works, Inc.
Santa Barbara, California 93160

The publisher grants the purchaser permission to reproduce the art in this book for classroom, school, or individual use. Reproduction for resale of any kind is strictly prohibited.

Printed in the United States of America.

Introduction

The Clip Art Carousel is a treasury of whimsical drawings designed to illustrate your words and enhance your messages. The drawings in this book have been called **All-Purpose Art** because they will serve all purposes in every season and can be used for any reason. They are grouped by subjects that include everything from slogans and symbols to robots and rockets and are readily adaptable to any occasion, professional or personal. A contents list on the inside of the back cover will help you locate the art you need to decorate your announcements, awards, bulletins, fliers, games, greeting cards, invitations, name tags, notes, place cards, posters, programs, or signs.

To use one of these drawings, photocopy the page on which it appears (so that the actual book page remains intact for later use), cut out the photocopy of the drawing you wish to use, attach it to the sheet you intend to decorate, and photocopy this sheet with the art in place. Clip art makes illustration easier and communication more creative.

Writing Devices

Slogans, Messages & Greetings

Slogans, Messages & Greetings

Awards

Flags, Banners & Balloons

The Clip Art Carousel: All-Purpose Art
© 1986 – The Learning Works, Inc.

Holidays & Seasons

8

Holidays & Seasons

Suns & Stars, Hearts & Flowers

Food

11

Animals

12

Animals

13

Birds, Bugs & Butterflies

Plants

15

Toys

Sports

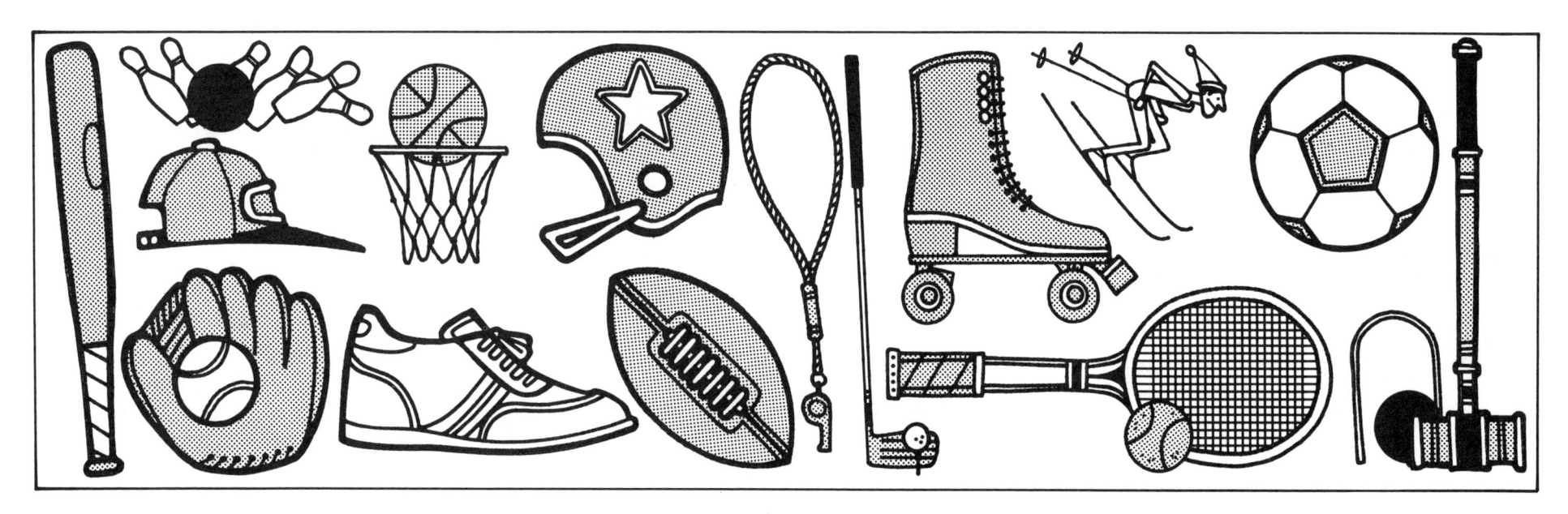

17

Music

18

On Stage

At the Circus

Careers

Careers

Pirates & Cowboys

Robots, Rockets & Space

Transportation

Buildings

26

Around the House

27

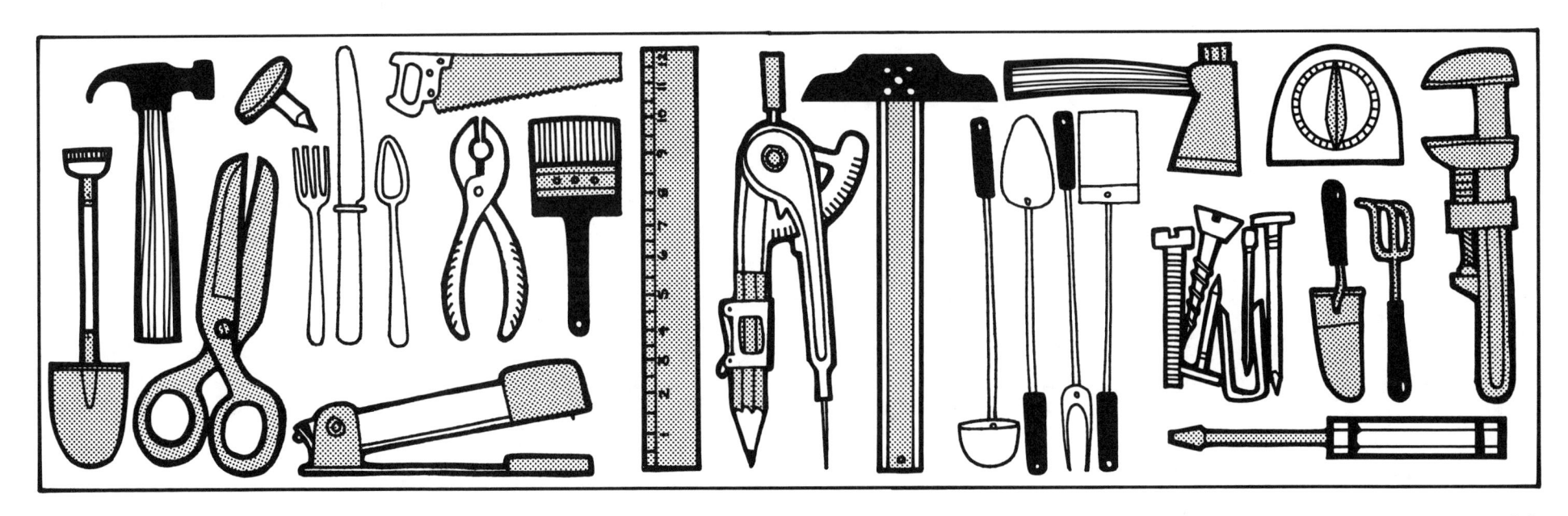

Tools & Gadgets

Signs & Symbols

Borders

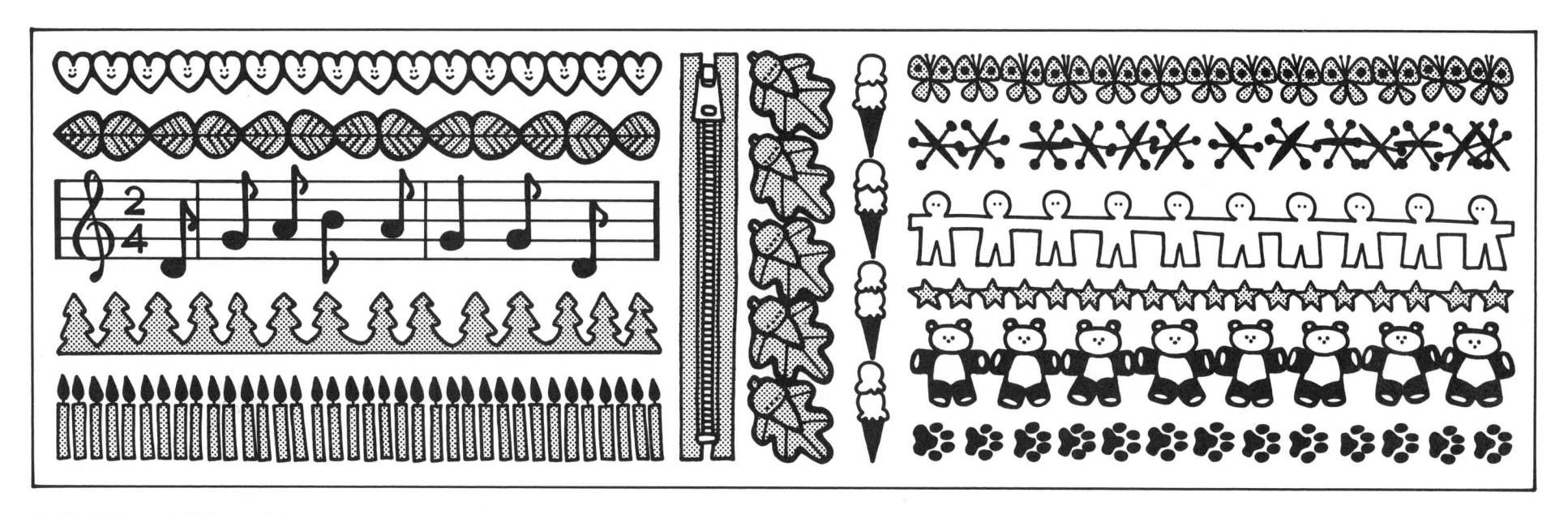

Borders

Borders

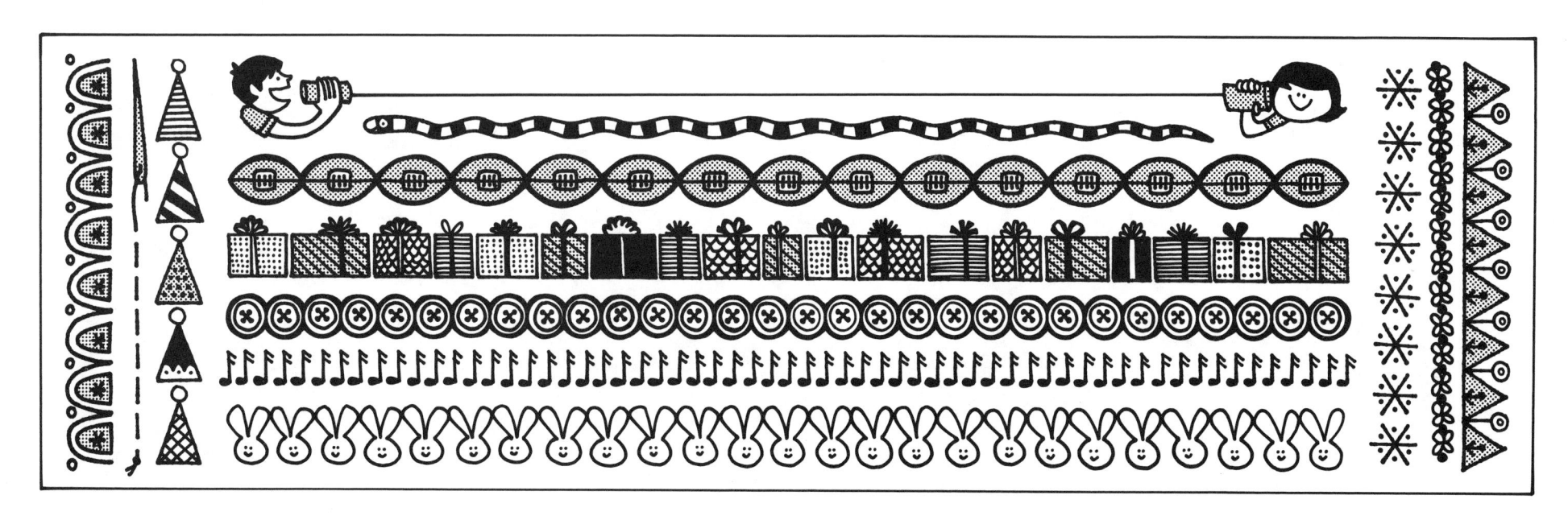